HOW
to
PRAY

ANDREW LEE SULLIVAN

ISBN 978-0-9980552-2-0 (ebook)
978-0-9980552-3-7 (paperback)

CONTENTS

INTRODUCTION

I'm writing about prayer only because Jesus says to do so. Each rising morning, he urges me to keep writing. After an early hour of prayer, I feel the presence of Jesus standing next to my bed. He simply says, "Andy, continue writing." He has his own purpose, I'm sure far beyond anything I can possibly imagine.

Wandering into the kitchen, I grab a cup of coffee and then scoot before the blank monitor and pray: "Jesus, what do you want to say today? Please say what you want to say!" The unorganized ideas flow and gradually take shape. Today, I'm starting to feel Jesus saying: "Andy, it's time to finish." So, here's a little book I truly didn't try to write. It seems it burst out of my heart simply when Jesus wanted. It's a glimpse of my prayer relationship with him.

I had a general sense that he wanted me to explain my prayer life. This book then, is misnamed. It's not so much an instruction on how to pray. It's more about how I pray. I'm sure that Jesus placed this book in your hands because he wants you to pray.

Who is this book for? That's a big question. It's easier to start with who this book is not for. If you're a theologian or prayer expert, this book is not so much for you. You already swim in the science and art of prayer. Hopefully, you shouldn't need my testimony to enjoy prayer. Nonetheless, I understand that a seemingly unsurmountable abyss may exist between theory and practice. If that's you, before reading, ask if you really believe in miracles and angels. Can't Jesus speak with a soul a bit differently than the norm?

This book is especially for anyone who is: hurt by the church, distant from God, lost, empty and purposeless, hopeless and despondent, angry at God, trapped in sin, abused and hiding, wounded by traumatic memories, unloved from childhood, or just hungry for something more in life. It's even for the believer who does not yet know the beauty and comfort of real prayer. If any of those descriptors fit you, keep reading.

You don't have to be a Christian or Catholic to open these pages. You can be a Jew, Muslim, Buddhist, Hindu, secular humanist, or atheist. Everyone is invited to meet Jesus, even the Satanists and witches. He beckons you to come. The only thing that matters is that you are willing to meet him.

I'm neither recruiting for a church, nor speaking for one. Voluntarily stepping away from the Catholic priesthood, I'm now like a leper to the structured church. Yet I distinguish: I'm not a leper to Jesus Christ. I'm forbidden by church hierarchy and canon lawyers to teach about Jesus through a formal ministry. But Jesus stands beside me, and inside me, smiling. By baptism, he commissions me to persuade the world to embrace him. He rescued me; how can I not shout about his love from the rooftops?

Long ago on almost consecutive mornings, Jesus twice drew a line on the floor in my bedroom. Each time, he dared me to step over the line to come to him. Each line represented a risk to me. The first was the risk of teaching about his love. The second was the risk of teaching absolutely anyone of any faith or persuasion. Each time, without any hesitation I flew over the line into Jesus' arms. Genuine love knows no risks! I couldn't jump fast enough over that line.

This is not the best book on prayer. And mine is not the best way to pray. But you need neither. You just need a personal way to talk with God better than your current conversation. So, take my hand and I'll walk you through a way. By the last page, you'll be holding Jesus' hand. That's more than enough.

For the kind-hearted Christian or the conscientious Catholic, a few essential notes must be added to alleviate anxieties or fears about praying differently.

There are many kinds of prayer. There are prayers of thanksgiving, praise, intercession, worship, repentance, and more. Prayers may be sung or spoken, communal or private, silent or verbalized, led by a minister, priest, prophet, healer, or pious layman. My way of prayer rejects none of these and complements them all. Each kind of prayer has its proper place and value in the Christian life. I share a way of private prayer that nurtures a personal and intimate friendship with Jesus.

The Bible is infinitely more important than this little book. If you truly want to know Jesus, read the Gospels of Matthew, Mark, Luke, and John. You'll discover him there, how he speaks, loves, leads, feels, thinks, knows everything, and works wonders. You'll witness how he died for your sins and rose from the tomb to save you. Mindful of this essential context, this little book aims to help you fall in love with the same Jesus Christ found in the Gospels. Merely understanding the historical Jesus falls short of living in his love.

1

REALITY

There are many prayer-gift rooms in heaven. Lost in prayer, I see angels abound at each of these colossal beehives of activity. Amazon fulfillment centers are toddler playrooms compared to these mighty epiphanies of God's creative goodness. A grand wrapping table rests immovably at a heightened stair climb in each bustling hub. Angels circle that table, wrapping presents around the clock. Never sleeping, they glimmer with God's radiance.

These angels wrap gifts of all shapes and colors, befitting the personal character, history, and natural inclination of each unique recipient. An ancient, massive book lays open in the center of each preparation table. This book lists the names of people down below on earth. Bathed in light, the book shows who is to receive a gift, and when. Momentarily, as they fold and seal, the angels consult the list.

After the gifts are wrapped, they're taken by passing angels and whisked away with haste. Each prayer-gift room is longer than a football field and higher than a telephone pole. Fine walls rise with lavish gold designs and marble pillars. Tens of thousands of gifts rest against every interior wall. But the heaps of gifts are more organized than they seem. The angels know the location of every personalized gift.

These gifts are breathtakingly extraordinary. Except for God Himself present in the world, these gifts are the most powerful realities on the planet. Among human beings there are no greater gifts granted by God than these. They are gifts of prayer, of the grace to bathe in God's presence and converse with uncreated Truth, Power, and Love Himself. Real prayer! What an astounding gift!

A prayer-gift imparts the knowledge, desire, inclination, facilitation, and habit of living in the intimate presence and friendship of Jesus Christ. It's a hidden and personal gift that grows beyond containment. It gradually, inevitably branches out and multiplies in countless surrounding souls. The intimacy and warmth of genuine prayer is wonderfully contagious.

Every now and then, I see a prayer-gift opened. Each time, the dazzling white and colored lights make me weep! It's hard not to cry when you witness overwhelming beauty. As the wrapping falls away, a pulsating ball of light enters the soul. The soul is never the same again. Love takes over.

Jesus has nurtured my grasp of prayer as a gift. In the Gospels he illustrates this gift in different ways. It's an inner wellspring of water gushing forth in the soul itself. It's a treasure discovered in a field, eagerly claimed by the purchase of that field. It's a tiny mustard seed that grows into a mighty tree. It's leaven in bread that makes the entire loaf expand.

These metaphors describe a personal, conversational relationship with Jesus that grows into his far-reaching presence throughout the whole world. Jesus uses metaphors to teach. Similarly, I use images to help hearts fall in love with Jesus. I'll explain that later. It hardly seemed like my own choice. I believe it was a gift imparted to my hopeless soul at the critical moment of my life.

Jesus desires to give every single person the gift of profound personal prayer. Of course, he accomplishes this by limitless modalities. One way is to rescue a lost man, transform him with love, give him the drive to spread love, and send him forth to give gifts of prayer to anyone and everyone. Imagine Santa Claus as always having prayer-gifts in the back of his vehicle. That's my story. I'm just one of many prayer-gift givers! I once met a crowd of them visiting heaven.

Although angels resolutely serve in the gift rooms above, these wonderful hubs of God's infinite-giving each operate under the leadership of a human person here on earth. Jesus loves to glorify men and women by working through them to give himself to the world. The angels are put into place to help. Anyway, I'm heavily involved now. Giving prayer-gifts is everything I live for.

Now it seems like ages ago when Jesus first walked me into my prayer-gift room. Over the high arched entrance, it read: "Todd's and Andy's Room." I was awestruck by the room's sheer size and beauty. Twelve gigantic angels stood around the central table. I felt so small and insignificant! Then Jesus introduced me to them and they shrank down to an almost "normal" size. The principal angel was named Lawrence and he welcomed me with a smile.

Without asking any questions, I intuitively understood two powerful truths: This was a sacred place that did exceedingly holy work; and the appealing packages were gifts of prayer for people on earth. I felt that this exhilarating room surpassed other angelic interventions. The following days, I'd ask many questions and learn a lot more.

One morning I stood there at the table with the angels. Jesus didn't seem to be around. I said, "I don't understand, am I here to help you deliver gifts or do you help me? Who helps who?" An angel immediately responded, "Oh no, we're the ones who help you." That seemed to make sense, as my name was on the room. I just wanted to figure things out.

The instant I wanted to know how to do this kind of work, Jesus appeared next to me and asked, "Would you like to meet Enoch?" I didn't see how Jesus' words were yet connected to the unspoken question in my mind. But the offer excited me and I answered "yes" right away. Then, from the back left corner of the room Enoch entered. I was dumbfounded. His intense, multi-colored rays of light stretched more plentiful and powerful than the angels. He appeared like a shining star. A flood of reflections bounced off the floor.

Enoch walked up to me and said, "All you need is to be holy. This is how God will lead people to you. This attracts them." Then he turned around and left. I felt so humbled and small and unworthy! Then I turned to the angels and said, "Who am I to do this!? I'm a nobody!" Jesus had his hand on my shoulder. Amused, the angels laughed a bit. They said, "You don't know who you are yet." I had a lot to learn.

I learned marvelous truths from Jesus and the angels assigned to me, way too much to explain at present. But the following must be shared. Whoever reads this, there is a gift for you. Don't pass it by. I'm praying that you receive your gift.

2

GOD'S SPECIAL GIFTS

G od lavishes personal gifts unique to each soul. A beautiful voice, for instance, mends broken hearts and restores estranged relationships. A profound intellect liberates ignorant minds. A skilled hand extends life with a transplanted heart. A creative propensity invents machines that bless everyone with convenience. The list of special gifts is almost endless. Every person has a special gift of one kind or another.

Each special gift is like a personal reservoir. God places it in the soul both for personal enrichment and for the betterment of others. It's neither like a lake that keeps everything for itself, nor like a river that empties itself and holds nothing for reserve. Rather, a person's special gift first fills the soul with its own goodness, and then overflows for the benefit of others.

God bestows spiritual gifts on believers too. Some have the gift of prophecy. Some read hearts. Some heal broken bodies with genuine miracles. Some preach eloquently with the dominion of God thundering behind every word. Each individual gift is providentially given for the benefit of the whole body of believers.

A special gift reveals the very meaning of a person's life. The better the gift is embraced, the better it unwraps a person's identity and destiny. Once the gift is realized, pursued, and developed, everything in life seems to click into place. "This is what God made me for!" Think of the greats: Noah building an ark; Moses leading a nation; Paul writing epistles; Patrick

Christianizing Ireland. God nourishes special gifts to sanctify and raise up the humbled, for his own mysterious far-reaching designs.

During the spring of 2020, Jesus began telling me who I am. Or better, I began listening earnestly. Now, at 60 years old; I'm finally discovering the ultimate purpose of why God created me. He birthed within me the special gift of intimate prayer and asked me to share it. I still have a long way to go, but I'm certain of his work in me. I know my special gift and mission.

3

A GIFT OF PERSONAL PRAYER

My own gift is humble, subtle, hidden, silent, calm, overlooked, presumed, and at times perhaps belittled by the mightily gifted. But of course, we can't all be climactic cymbalists in the ensemble. Soft, heart-pulling violin strings are needed, too. That's me. I'm neither a dramatic healer, nor a mind-blowing prophet, nor a mesmeric visionary. My special gift is a kind heart with the diamond of intimate prayer. So simple.

From my youth, God gave me a friendly, helpful, and gentle heart. But any natural endowment requires a supernatural orientation to flourish eternally. Without that orientation, a special gift can tend to harm. Picture a twelve-year-old in the driver's seat of the luxurious Bentley. Although my life started with a good heart, that natural starting point was not enough to fill me and selflessly overflow.

God had to step into my life to "upgrade my heart" with something abundantly worthy to receive and give away. He gave me his close friendship, his abiding love, his presence, himself. My natural gift now thrives with a supernatural purpose, modality, and power behind it. There's a world of difference between sharing natural love and bursting at the seams with supernatural love.

This "heart-upgrade" boils down to an extraordinary way of prayer. My special gift is praying in images. Some pray in tongues. Others pray in a crowd, merged in a sea of swaying hands. Still others need incense and Latin chant to faintly brush heaven. These paths of prayer may work for others. But I'm just not there. I merely pray in images, all alone in my bedroom.

Yes, I'm different! My "heart-upgrade" demanded a great price though, requiring many restless and lost years before I stumbled onto my way of prayer. It entered my life only after great suffering. I'll get to the blood, sweat, and tears later. First, I'll describe and clarify my gift.

4

Praying with the Help of Images

How do I pray? I close my eyes and imagine a scene where Jesus and I meet. It could be a seashore, a blossoming park, or a cozy mountainside cabin. I imagine what I see, hear, smell, touch, taste. Taking my time to paint the picture, I escape until I see, feel, my presence there. Jesus then approaches me in this "prayer-template," as it were. Such an opening scene is the beginning of an intimate interaction with him.

With a big grin on his face, I see Jesus walk up to me. Ever so comfortable, he gives me a warm hug and asks how I'm doing. He's happy to see me and shows it with a familiar smile. Jesus' full attention settles upon me and I can see unconditional love flashing in his eyes.

He sees straight into my heart and knows me. Sitting comfortably with him, a quiet enjoyment of his presence may be enough. He may hold my hand as we contemplate the ocean and enjoy the dancing sun on the sparkling waters. He truly listens and truly speaks, sometimes in words. Other times he converses with his own suggested images. Above all else, I see and even feel his loving and accepting presence.

Over a hot cup of coffee, I've enjoyed many early mornings with Jesus in a comfy booth in a café tucked away somewhere in Tennessee. Sometimes with rain pouring down outside a grand window, we've leisurely chatted about practically everything. We laugh, reveal our secrets, complain, wish, share our feelings, and trust each other. Over time, we've bonded as genuine, intimate friends!

Any other day, Jesus takes hold of my hand and walks me into a traumatic memory in my life. With him standing next to me, we view the details of the tragedy. It's hard to revisit the mess and I cry a lot. But I didn't start it! He just grabbed hold of my hand and led me there. I had no idea where we were going.

After repeated mornings of prayer like this, the emotional upheaval eventually recedes, and then it happens. I discover Jesus actually there in that memory and witness his loving presence seen in that past event. I see him and understand his purpose. I see his unconditional love there. Was the memory changed? No, he simply revealed a critical piece of past veiled reality: himself. His invisible presence was there all along, suddenly made clear. Penetrating healing!

After many such prayer experiences, I no longer have any traumatic memories. They're all gone! Whenever I remember my worst emotional traumas in life, I see Jesus there and am filled with gratitude. I understand the beautiful mystery of suffering. All my amassed suffering in life was well worth the torrent of love in my heart today.

After nearly 1,500 hours of prayer, you can only imagine where I've been, what I've seen, what I've heard from the lips of Jesus. We've watched my birth, and his. He whisked me away to see heaven many times. I've learned amazing things there. We've even walked around inside my soul. Talk about learning! We've spent many hours with his Father and Holy Spirit too, all three Divine Persons surrounding the bed, exploding in blinding light. A lot of tears, humbly beholding in awe the mystery and beauty of God!

5

STEP-BY-STEP PROCEDURE

1. Imagine a beautiful place.

2. Using your senses, find your comfort and peace in that place.

3. Notice Jesus, who approaches and greets you with familiarity and pleasure.

4. See how Jesus treats you, how completely present he is to you, how he loves you unconditionally.

5. Simply receive his love and enjoy his presence.

6. As with your best friend, speak to him from your heart, with no formality or mask wearing.

7. See how he listens and responds; listen to him.

6

THE PRAYER OF PRESENCE

With all that said, what is this crazy experience of praying with images? What's really going on here? I've spent years pondering this question. Is it just me in my head or God and his revelation? Like dreams, is it merely the projections of my subconscious? Is it lively intuitive thought or a real encounter with Jesus? Bottom line: I believe it's all of this.

It's prayer. It's a real conversation between Jesus and me. Some images and thoughts come from me; others come from Jesus. We converse using images. He knows the thoughts and images of my soul and responds with his own thoughts and images. The whole experience is a mixture of what comes from me and what comes from him. After all, I'm not an angel. Why shouldn't God talk to me as a human being? It's the dance of two minds mingling, while each move independently, too.

Such "image conversation" between God and man shouldn't be surprising. The Bible is packed with instances of God speaking to souls through prophecies, visions, stories, and dreams. Communicative images! Jesus loved to paint the imagery of his parables in the minds of his listeners. Images are a profoundly human way to communicate. Imagine commercials, movies, analogies, novels, paintings, emojis. Images hit hard in the soul and reverberate forever. By images, God accommodates for our feeble and slow grasp of the truth.

Besides, Jesus taught that we should love God with our whole heart, mind, soul, and strength. Now apply this to prayer. When I love God with my whole heart, I love him with all my sentiments, desires, will, affections, dreams, feelings, and images within me. We should not be afraid of approaching God as real human beings. Wouldn't it help to connect with Jesus by feeling his hand in your own hand? Isn't this a simple way of loving God with my whole heart?

I understand that whatever is imagined is not real. But consider, words in themselves are not real, either. Have you ever actually seen and touched a living and breathing word? Although I can pet a dog, I can't pet the word "dog." No, both expressed words and imagined images are symbols. But they do serve to connect us with the realities they symbolize.

For instance, when I imagine sitting next to Jesus at the beach, holding hands with him; I'm not really there. Everything is just in my head. Oh, but there's more to it. Although the image is unreal, it both symbolizes and connects me with the real.

The divine person of Jesus is real and he's truly present to me, extending his love. The image makes this abstract and invisible truth very real to me. It opens the eyes of my soul to Jesus already present. I come to know his presence by a human experience that enriches my faith and reason. I move beyond knowing about Jesus to actually meeting him, even in my feelings.

For years, I'd been searching for the best description of this kind of prayer. At times, I called it "Baby Meditation," or "Therapeutic Prayer," or "Affirmation Meditation." But everything seemed to elusively escape its essential definition. Then one beautiful day on the beach, Jesus turned to me and casually said, "Andy, call it the Prayer of Presence." Yes, of course, that's it!

With this kind of prayer, the imagination is used as a steppingstone leading to God's presence. It diminishes distractions and helps the soul focus on Jesus. Imagining Jesus, I soon come to experience not an imagined presence, but the actual and immediate presence of Jesus. The image then merely serves a grounding and focusing purpose. The experience of Jesus' real presence is the heartbeat of the prayer.

In practice, the Prayer of Presence proceeds like this: In a calm environment where interior stillness is possible, I imagine a beautiful scene. I then imagine meeting Jesus there. I get lost in our presence and conversation. I see how much he accepts me. I passively receive his unconditional love. I gradually grow into an intimate friendship with him.

7

TRYING TO UNDERSTAND THE PRAYER OF PRESENCE

1. Seeing Jesus present to me and seeing how much he loves me is the heartbeat of this prayer.

2. Seeing is believing.

3. Jesus not only knows my thoughts; he sees the images moving within my soul and takes it from there.

4. Jesus speaks not only by words, but by images; consider instances of prophecy and dreams in the Bible.

5. He assumes his limitless freedom and power to suggest a desired direction; "leading the dance."

6. This prayer has a life of its own, the mind and heart of God at work within me.

7. It's personal prayer, an informal conversation with God, where he acts as the protagonist.

8. The prayer's image is not real, but it symbolizes drawing me deeper into reality, not further away.

9. A childlike faith is the prerequisite for such prayer; truly a precious treasure only revealed to the humble.

10. The journey begins with receiving love, growth and healing follow, and eventually giving love blossoms.

11. It's not reading, thinking, speaking, introspecting, moralizing; but seeing, whispering, listening, loving.

12. It does not focus on *doing* but *being*.

13. Start with a simple plan and apply the senses; when love happens, the method gives way to spontaneity.

14. Contact with Jesus' presence and the passive reception of his love is everything in this kind of prayer.

15. After many years of familiarity, I tend to become like Jesus because he is living with me and within me.

16. Each kind of prayer has its value; this prayer nurtures intimacy and enriches every other kind of prayer.

17. It needs a distraction-free environment and internal stillness to practice.

18. It takes courage and a daily commitment.

8

FIND A WAY TO MAKE THIS PRAYER YOUR OWN

1. Besides the prayer, seek to know the person of Jesus in the Gospels.

2. Give this Prayer of Presence a test run, and then decide if you want to pursue it in your life.

3. Set a distraction-free time and place for this prayer in your daily schedule.

4. Make a serious commitment to devote a year to this kind of daily prayer.

5. Perhaps soft music, a picture, a burning candle, or the smell of incense may help.

6. Keep a journal and write down your Prayer of Presence experiences.

7. If there's a friend who might travel this spiritual path with you, that would be encouraging.

8. Nurture a lifestyle that increases your exposure to goodness and beauty.

9

GOD'S TEACHING NICHE

That's enough entry-level stuff. This explains my special gift in a nutshell. Now God can really start writing! Let's return to the analogy of the reservoir. The special gift first fills and enriches a person, and then overflows to others. I've agonized about how to explain this. I could write a book about it. There's so much to say, but I can't find a way to even scratch the surface. Such was the disjointed puzzle in my brain when I fell asleep last night. Where and how to write next?

Three hours later, I woke at 1:15 am. Whenever I wake so early, I customarily ask Jesus to let me sleep a little more so I might pray better later. Seems reasonable. Sometimes it works, sometimes it doesn't. This morning I soon felt him urging me to get up and pray. He stood beside the bed, and I quickly filled with energy. After the first prayer of the day for my wife, as always, I turned to him and said, "Jesus, tell me what to write!"

Prayer time. I closed my eyes and found myself comfortably sitting with the Father, Son, and Holy Spirit. I did not plan this image; it seemed to unexpectedly rush into my soul. We relaxed in a cozy niche, seated in comfy chairs spread out before a dancing and crackling fire. The logs needed attention. An angel came by, added some pieces of wood, and stoked the fire. Other angels behind us moved about as they pleased.

The Father was dressed in a royal purple robe with wavy gold patters swirling around. He kept a mature white beard and caring face, and greeted me with a warm nod. Without the slightest hesitation, I kissed him on the cheek before I sat down. It felt familiar for both of us. Without words, radiating stability, he smiled.

The Holy Spirit was to the left of the Father. He glistened in splendor, sending forth white and colored rays of light. He manifested as the translucent figure of a beautiful, luminous man. I could see him yet see through him. But his chair remained empty. It seemed he felt more himself to hover about, full of moving energy. There was a holy restlessness about him. He touched me with a transitory but kind greeting.

Jesus sat to my right, enjoying the fire. His glorious countenance is so handsome! Our presence to each other felt distinct from my encounters with the Father and the Holy Spirit. It was like we'd been close friends for a thousand years. We felt our history together. Imagine an aging couple married for 50 years, still holding hands, still with enduring love in their sparkling eyes. Something like that. We bonded with a profound, familiar, mutual understanding. The comfort of our intimacy made me euphoric, yet calm. I could have soaked there in joy for another thousand years.

I said we were all together in a cozy niche. I know the exact place; we've been there many times. But to appreciate it, you need a wider glimpse of the room where the niche situates.

My prayer-gift room in heaven. Imagine the magnificent interior space about the length of a football field, half that in width. Marbled pillars and ornate gold patterns majestically decorate towering walls. The floor is amazing! It's a worn but smooth expanse of crystal tiles. It emanates a dozen colors depending on your viewing angle. It's either opaque or transparent according to your interest. If you merely desire, you stand firmly upon the surface. Wish otherwise, and you effortlessly pass through the floor and soar down to earth below.

Usually, there's a lot of angelic activity in this room. In the center, there's an enormous, elevated table with a grand canopy. Twelve "gift angels" wrap gifts there. Their role is to help facilitate the delivery of prayer-gifts for broken souls. "Battle angels" occupy the far-left side of the room. They assist the overall effort by fighting resistance to the delivery or reception of the gifts. "Word-of-knowledge angels" help convince skeptics to take a step of faith and welcome the gifts. It's a busy place, angels flying through the floor around the clock, gifts in hand.

It's a humbling place to visit. I often cry when I'm there, feeling so unworthy to even be a part of such a work of God. Have you ever walked around in St. Peter's Basilica in Rome? I've probably been there a hundred times, always struck by the sheer power and beauty of the place. Well, that room feels like nothing compared to my gift room in heaven.

Thousands and thousands of exquisitely wrapped gifts of all shapes and colors hug the walls all around. This shows that each gift is unique and personalized, prepared perfectly for the recipient. The room is packed everywhere. This shows that there is a great amount of work as I move toward the future.

The niche is located where a long stretch of gifts parts in the middle of the right wall, establishing an area to take a rest from intense periods of work. There's a gorgeous rug, plush leather chairs, and a charming fireplace always burning. A coffee table and reading lamp complete this "break room," so to speak. Mind you, the angels don't need this niche. It's me that gets tired. Jesus granted me this room long ago and put me in charge. He's been teaching me how to work with the angels ever since.

The niche also serves as a meeting place. Jesus uses it to teach me whatever I'm ready to know. All good things in time. He and I have experienced critical meetings in that niche, that keep changing my life happily irreversibly. Today would be such an encounter. Remember? Upon awakening I plainly stated, "Jesus, tell me what to write!" Sometimes we say things to God loosely without much thought. But he listens to every movement of the heart and answers profoundly. He shot me right to the niche.

So, here we are: the Father, Son, Holy Spirit, and me, sitting around the fire. Unexpectedly, Jesus rises and takes a few steps to face me directly. He bends down and kneels before me and silently indicates for me to stretch out my feet. I don't know what's going on, but follow his prompt. He then pours water over my feet and washes them. He then dries my feet and returns to his chair. It all takes place in silence, except for the sound of moving water and crackling fire. My mind races.

I felt that Jesus was teaching me how to give the gift. I should do the same. I should humbly serve those he sends my way. His example shows me how to give the Prayer of Presence. Yet after reflecting, I believe there's something more. He's telling me not to proudly claim credit for my gift. I'm to let it overflow to others, ultimately as *his* gift. The cleansing waters and fire of the Spirit are not my own, but his. My role is to be a humble instrument, letting Jesus give the gift from within me. I'm trying to understand.

10

A MEETING DESIGNED IN HEAVEN

H e's back in his chair now, enjoying the fire. Jesus glances in my direction and asks me, "Andy, do you remember the day I rescued you?" I remember it well. All the richness of it! It's permanently etched in my memory. I respond, "Yes, I do." I feel a surge of gratitude. Then Jesus calmly says: "Everything you need to say is there." He's telling me how to explain the overflow of the gift. He's completing the puzzle, answering the prayer. He doesn't need to say anything else.

My mind instantly fled to that memory. You'll want critical background information here. You can't appreciate a rescue until you understand the despair of captivity. Jesus wanted me to tell the whole ugly and beautiful story. No surprise, he loved to teach by stories. Nonetheless, I'll try to abbreviate.

I closed my eyes, and I was there. It was 2005, a rainy October morning in Rogers Park, Illinois. I was a Catholic priest at that time, temporarily living in a house a stone's throw from Lake Michigan. My General Superior had sent me to that residence for a couple months, to provide the sacraments for the members of a religious community. With a few hours' notice, my stay abruptly ended. I had to pack like lightning and catch a flight from O'Hare to Rome, Italy. No true explanation was given, just a command to return home.

Once my General Superior had come to his senses, he realized the mistake he'd made sending me to Chicago. He addressed his mistake by demanding my immediate return. Someone had to accompany me too, in case I might attempt to escape. I lived under house arrest and could not leave the property. This is how I existed in Rome; the same restrictions applied in Rogers Park. I was a house prisoner, restrained by a letter warning that I'd go to hell if I disobeyed. Back in Rome, the judgment prevailed that I should never have been allowed to travel to the United States. Either place was the same. I lived fenced in by interior walls, with my passport locked in a safe.

Meanwhile, several days before rushing to O'Hare airport, a priest from Puerto Rico visited that Rogers Park residence. He shouldn't have been there, either. He had tried to get a direct flight from San Juan to Phoenix, but reluctantly took a layover in Chicago. It was cheaper. His travels were just as erratic as mine. He'd been hurriedly instructed by Rome to get to Phoenix as soon as possible. This priest, Father Mike Dietrich, ended up staying at the Rogers Park residence for a few days. He was shocked to see me there!

That improbable crossing of our paths still reverberates in my life. Flawed human authorities had exercised their ridiculous government over Mike and me. But God quietly intervened for his own purpose. The crossing of our paths resulted in the most important meeting of my life. The moment of my rescue! We met by chance, but God had certainly arranged it.

I'd known Father Mike for many years. At various times I had lived with him in Chicago; Avila, Spain; and Rome, Italy. Emotionally and psychologically, he suffered from an extremely traumatic past. Imagine PTSD! His own father and the General Superior in Rome for many years abused him with heightened cruelty. And although he had the natural gift of remarkable intelligence, he was an emotional basket case. He lived in an internal cloud of fear, despair, and nerve-racking anxiety. Severe rejection was written on his face.

Meeting Mike, I immediately noticed that he was different. Something had changed inside of him; I could see the calm of inner peace in his eyes. His glance was now clear. The familiar blank, lonely, dull stare was gone. Now a smile, not forced but truly genuine! I could sense happiness and confidence in his voice. This was not the same Fr. Mike Dietrich I once knew. The way he gave me his attention was now from the heart, undivided, without self-interest. Wow! What happened?

Soon after arriving at the house, Mike approached me privately; "Andy,

whenever you have time, I'd like to get together with you and talk a little."
I distractedly agreed, unaware that for many months he'd been praying for
me and waiting for the day to see me. Somehow, Jesus had finally brought
us face to face. Wasting no time, Mike seized the opportunity. He'd received
the gift of praying with the help of images and wanted to share it. He knew
I desperately needed this kind of prayer. But he'd have to introduce me to
it and convince me to try it. If it had transformed him so profoundly, he
thought it surely could help me.

11

JUST THE MEETING

Before focusing on the unseen and spiritual dimension of my rescue, the historical account of my meeting with Father Mike Dietrich should be told. We'll start with the facts of our actual conversation. After this groundwork, we'll then move on to unveil God's invisible hand at work in rescuing me. Here's what I remember:

I closed the door and Mike and I situated ourselves across from each other, separated by a stylish coffee table. A ceramic vase with fresh daises sat on a crocheted white doily. Father Mike relaxed on a comfortable couch, while I pulled up a wicker-worked chair. Our feet rested on an old parquet floor, shamelessly dulled by the ravages of bleach. As the world roared by, our words froze in time, marking the dramatic ending and beginning of my history. If there was a key turning point in my life, this was it.

We asked how each other were doing, first chit chatting about the shutting down of Puerto Rico. Mike lamented the loss of the peace and quiet he had enjoyed on the island. I then related the weird way I'd ended up in Chicago. Past the preliminaries, Father Mike launched into the depths.

"Andy, I've wanted to have this meeting with you for a long time, for about six months. Nobody asked me to meet with you. This is just between us. I had no idea when we'd be able to sit down and talk." Now he looked serious.

I felt relieved that the meeting was Mike's initiative. Assured that

Duran (the General Superior in Rome) was not behind it, I lowered my guard and became open to what Mike wanted to say. Duran often spoke through puppets and employed them to gather evidence against his targets. I'd often played the role of spying on community members for him.

"It hurts me to know how cruelly you've been treated. I cried when I heard of Duran's harsh dealing with you," he said. Mike put it politely. "I know the despair that comes from such treatment. I've been treated the same way for years."

Suddenly, spontaneously, Father Mike broke down in front of me. Emotion flooded into his face and tears ran down his cheeks. He cried at the injustice and cruelty of it all. Shaking his head in disbelief, Mike let his heart go.

"How useless it is to help anyone by humiliations, insults, and intimidations. It's useless! Totally useless! Now, I'm assigned to recruit vocations. For what? I don't want candidates to experience what I wouldn't wish on my worst enemies."

It felt awkward to hear a member of our religious community speak this way. I tried to appear non-committal, but inside I agreed wholeheartedly.

After Mike wiped the tears from his eyes and blew his nose, he gathered his composure and introduced the substance of our conversation.

"Andy, I know what is wrong with you." He paused and looked directly at me.

"I believe that you have emotional deprivation disorder. I've known you for many years and I now understand this disorder. Maybe it's not full blown in you, but it's there. It's fully curable, and I know how to help."

Hanging on every word, I had no idea what he was talking about. He continued.

"Emotional deprivation disorder is a state of emotional retardation. It's experienced unsuspectingly by many adults. Of the two categories of human emotions, the heartfelt and softer emotions, such as desire, joy, tenderness, empathy, affection and love, are frozen in a non-developed state. Subsequently, lacking the support of these softer emotions, the other set of assertive or doing-oriented emotions take over. These emotions, such as hope, courage, audacity, anger, fear, anxiety, overdevelop. I know that's a mouthful to say, but the disorder boils down to a lopsided state of thinking and feeling. In a nutshell: the love-experiencing side of a person is stuck in infancy or childhood; the action side is jammed into high gear."

Wondering if this condition applied to me, I squirmed a little and asked the obvious question.

"Okay, so what's the cause of this disorder? How does a person end up lopsided?"

"It's caused by a deprivation of mature and affirming love during the early years of life. This mature love is characterized by its unconditional and unselfish quality. Naturally lavished by parents, it's expressive and experienced by the infant or child in a healthy sensual way. It's absorbed by the beloved through the mother's facial expressions, hugs, kisses, caresses, and various signs of acceptance. As this love is progressively soaked up by the developing child, a virtual emotional nursing and growing occurs. This inherent process strengthens and makes firm the emotional and later psychological dimensions of the person. As such, quality love passively received creates an emotionally complete adult."

The rain intensified outside the window. The whitewashed radiator clicked, and another round of heating started up. Oblivious to the subtle sound of an old radiator, Mike barreled ahead. "A deprivation of such love results in the crimping of a natural developmental process. Without the freely flowing love I've described, a frustration or deprivation ensues, robbing the person of the indispensable emotional food he or she must receive to emotionally mature.

"A parent may have radiated no feelings of love or demonstrated hatred for an infant and this would cause a deep deprivation. But it's enough that parental love is defective, lacking expression, weak or selfish for a less severe deprivation to occur. Or it may be enough that love is present but not subjectively experienced by the child, for the adult in later years to suffer the frustrating effects of deprivation."

He paused to inhale, and I jumped in with a question.

"So, if a deprivation of love stops the softer emotions from developing, how is this related to the overdevelopment of the action-oriented emotions?"

Mike seemed to know the answer to every question.

"When love is withheld at the existential level, the person eventually experiences a difficulty establishing a genuinely felt emotional rapport with other adults. Deep seated feelings of non-acceptance, non-belonging, insecurity, and inadequacy prevail. As the emotionally unaffirmed adult feels misunderstood, relationship fears grow, and heartfelt friendships become elusive. The unaffirmed come to feel that they have no place in an emotionally tough adult world, where they feel like children. This internal disconnect then spills over into the external social life. Here, the assertive emotions either compensate by driven activity to win love and acceptance, or recoil in fear." Without skipping a beat, Mike scooped up a dog-eared paperback book near his right hand.

"In short, when the softer emotions stop growing, the assertive side of a person strives to fill the gap and survive."

Mike's volume of knowledge and precision of distinctions seemed encyclopedic, at least to me. The guy was a brain in a wheelbarrow, something I'd always admired about him.

Outside, the heavens burst open, and a downpour hit the streets. Inside, a similar scene was going on in my head.

Mike next detailed the historic origins of emotional deprivation disorder and the story of the doctors who had pioneered its definition and therapy.

Dr. Anna Terruwe of the Netherlands and Dr. Conrad Baars, who had survived the Nazis' Buchenwald concentration camp, identified the symptomology of the condition and tweaked an original salutary approach.

As Mike rapid-fired the particulars, I began to search within and suddenly realized the truth of it all. I had the symptoms he described: father-hunger, a people-pleasing disposition, workaholic tendencies, oversensitivity, difficulties in establishing and feeling adult friendships, deep seated insecurities, mask-wearing to hide my true feelings.

More than that, Mike was different now, less controlled by fear, warm hearted, empathetic, loving. Something had changed him. I could see happiness in his eyes. His new demeanor convinced me; his long explanations hinted at a successful path he'd traveled.

"Mike," I interrupted him. "Can we go to the cure? How is emotional deprivation disorder cured?" It was a personal question now.

The once broken priest momentarily paused. A discernable satisfaction accented his face. My eyes must have said it all. I really wanted the answer. All along, he wanted to get to praying with images.

Leaning forward, he began.

"Terruwe and Baars devised a psychotherapeutic treatment that proved remarkably successful in their clinical practice. It stemmed from a simple premise: a frustrated natural process resumes its development once the proper conditions of growth are restored. Accordingly, they allowed their patients to finally experience the mature, affirming, and expressive love they had missed during the early years of life. In such a generative environment, monitored by reason, the softer emotions grew, and the assertive emotions mitigated until a state of emotional balance persisted. They called this treatment 'affirmation therapy.' By a loving presence, passively received, the therapy effected emotional maturity. This kind of therapy is distinct from the ordinary psychotherapies aimed at correcting repressive disorders."

The answer both encouraged and discouraged me. I frowned, dropped my eyes and shook my head. Nothing good ever happens. Yes, there was a real cure, but it existed on a fairy tale island a million miles away. My heart sank. How could I possibly go to psychotherapy? How could I find the right psychotherapist? And the money? Duran would never permit any of this nonsense.

Mike perceived my changing attitude as a sudden wave of pessimism and doubt swept over me.

"Andy, there's a way to replace clinical affirmation therapy with a therapeutic kind of meditation."

"Meditation?" I could hardly fathom this. I needed therapy, not prayer.

"Yes," Mike replied. "And who could better assume the role of a psychotherapist, then the Divine Physician himself, Jesus Christ?"

"Okay, I understand that." I grasped it in theory, not in practice. "I'm doubtful. I've been practicing meditation for twenty-six years with no therapeutic benefit. There's hardly any spiritual benefit."

I didn't explain the miserable state of my soul and the impossible gulf that separated God and me. Father Mike smiled and described the radical new direction of his prayer life: "I replaced years of almost fruitless and dry intellectual considerations with vividly imagined encounters with Jesus Christ."

Wait a minute. Still pursuing the treatment for the disorder, I frowned and resisted the idea of meditation as a therapeutic substitute. "I don't understand the connection between meditation and the healing of emotional deprivation disorder. Can a homemade remedy really replace professional therapy?"

"The essential element of a cure is the passive reception of mature love," Mike continued. "This love is experienced in the senses and emotions, and then makes its way to the mind. Through the power of the imagination, which is closely linked with the sensual and emotional powers, the loving presence of Jesus can be felt and absorbed into the psyche, producing therapeutic effects."

Though I was still skeptical, Mike's profound transformation made me think twice.

"Okay Mike, how do you do this?"

"The gains I've experienced in prayer were despite the community. Discard your malformation regarding meditation, its systemic obsessions of fear, exacting accountability, self-analysis, self-improvement, and intellectual cherry picking."

Mike had just jettisoned the pillars of my prayer life.

"Andy, 'affirmation meditation' is simply imagining Jesus loving you. You see and breathe and touch a comfortable setting, such as a seashore or forest, and find peace and relaxation there. Then, you imagine Jesus with you. You experience His loving gaze and touch. You witness his loving responses to your feelings, dreams, discouragements, likes, thoughts, memories, and daily occurrences. Everything is spontaneous. The emphasis is placed on the passive reception of love, not on what you can or should do, not even on understanding."

He explained more, encouraged me to read a book by Terruwe and Baars *(Healing the Unaffirmed)*, and urged me to commit myself to trying this prayer. Seeing my hesitancy, Mike implored me to promise that I'd read the book and give the prayer a chance. I gave him my word and he visibly leaned backward in relief. Mike had accomplished his self-appointed mission.

The rain had come and gone. The room seemed brighter. The aged radiator had sputtered and clacked off a while ago. A couple of hours had vanished. The workday beckoned. White daises stretched upward in the foreground, a calm, happy-faced priest made his own promise.

"Andy, the meditation I've described is extremely powerful. It will tend to take on a life all its own. You'll see for yourself. In about fifteen months you'll feel loved so intensely, you'll beg God to lessen it."

Of everything said, that single statement moved me the most. I wanted to experience that kind of love. A spark of courage ignited in my soul.

We rose from our journey and stretched our legs, as if we'd been confined in a compact car. I thanked Mike more than once. We hugged and he pledged his prayers for me. Within a few days, Father Mike Dietrich would dash to Phoenix and my life would never be the same.

12

Gift for a Broken Soul

oving beyond the material account of that meeting, the spiritual
realities remained veiled. Mike had little idea of the depth of my
spiritual bankruptcy. I sat there and listened, but my heart was
far, far away from God. A person can take only so much suffering before
he or she breaks. After years of despair and wishing to die, my insides felt
shattered to pieces. Only the fear of hell kept me from suicide. My soul
wished for any kind of accident that would end my life.

Beyond hopeless, I survived in an internal state of despondency. Finally,
I no longer cared about anything. I neither hoped for genuine love from
another human being, nor from God. Life had destroyed me. It was over.
I truly felt that God had abandoned me. Mike kept talking. Skeptical, I
politely listened. Yet his transformed face slowly worked on me.

Although I still believed in God, I no longer believed in God's love for
me. Such abstract theology only confused me. I knew it but did not feel
it. Life had been reduced to a meaningless grasping to endure. Just hang
on. While I wore a public mask of productivity and compliance, my real
interests focused on avoiding the next round of false accusations, insults,
and public humiliations.

I lived in a cult and didn't know it. The cult leader was a sociopath, and
I was his primary target of shame and psychological abuse, privately and
publicly. I was trapped in the orbit of this General Superior's damaging

dysfunctionality and toxic environment. I'd been indoctrinated and brain-washed and had no idea. I was in the middle of a house confinement that would last almost three and a half years. Fear paralyzed me.

If that wasn't enough, I was also emotionally retarded, and completely unaware of this condition. My fundamental emotional dispositions and tendencies were defective. I suffered from an insufficiently developed emotional life. My emotional capacity to feel and enjoy love and friendship was frustrated. I couldn't experience the genuine comfort of emotional joy and happiness. Imagine a life without knowing the feeling of having a friend! Rather, my emotional pattern was locked into overdrive as I habitually grasped at acceptance by achievement.

But there was more than physical captivity, despair, fear, psychological abuse, and a devastating emotional syndrome. Having turned away from hope in God, I'd surrendered to the pleasure of sin as a way out of misery. But my powerless dependencies on pornography, masturbation, and alcohol abuse, only served to intensify my grief. My mind was constantly preoccupied with how to steal money, sneak out of the house, buy what my heart couldn't live without, and squirrel it away somewhere. Anxiety ruled over me.

My days were packed full of menial jobs. I lived like Cinderella without a happy ending in sight: cooking, washing dishes, cleaning, washing and folding laundry, ironing, writing fundraising letters, teaching others how to fundraise, fixing anything broken. The list seemed endless. The best part of each day was popping a triple dose of Tylenol and drifting off to sleep. I'd imagine gripping a gun beneath my pillow. Like a teddy bear, this imagined weapon soothed me with security and comfort. Then I could fall asleep. Waking was terrible. Another day to be afraid all over again.

Truthfully, real prayer could have solved everything. I was a Catholic priest who'd lived in a spiritual institute extolled for making people saintly. But I did not yet know how to truly pray. In practice, prayer was reduced to mindlessly pronouncing Latin, introspecting, examining the conscience, studying from a religious book, check-marking resolutions, begging for help, conforming my actions to the fulfillment of my duties, reading the Bible—anything but truly falling in love with the person of Jesus. I really didn't want to talk to him, anyway.

My prayer was all about learning and doing and had nothing to do with passively receiving. Tragically, I had missed everything that was important about prayer. Prayer was lost in a world of effectivity, blind to the experience of simply meeting Jesus, hand in hand, toe to toe, face to face, eye to eye, heart to heart. I didn't know about this world. I knew nothing about prayer.

Sure, I'd heard a thousand times that prayer is a conversation with God. I did know some theology. I just didn't know how to live it. Cult indoctrination had filled my head with all kinds of wrong ideas about prayer.

13

RECEIVING THE GIFT

I was a broken man! That was the real me sitting across from Father Mike that rainy Chicago morning in the autumn of 2005. I remember the whole scene. I still see it all. Later in life, Jesus and I returned to this scene many times in prayer. Each time we observed, I gradually saw more and more reality. I saw Jesus superimposed in Mike. I saw a multitude of gifts overflowing into the hallway. I saw angels moving about, and an angel standing next to Mike holding a beautifully wrapped gift for me.

Mike wanted a "yes" from me. That's all he wanted, just that I'd try this new way of prayer.

"Andy, the meditation I've described is extremely powerful. It will tend to take on a life all its own. You'll see for yourself. In about fifteen months you'll feel loved so intensely, you'll beg God to lessen it."

Of everything said, that single statement moved me the most. I wanted to experience that kind of love.

Finally, I said, "Okay, I'll try it." Skeptical, I figured I'd nothing to lose. There was neither magic, nor flashes of light, nor epiphanies, nor warm fuzzy feelings. Nothing changed visually, but my eternity changed. Ultimately, it was Mike's happy face that convinced me to accept this new way of prayer. I had no idea that my "yes" would be the most important moment of my life.

Later, the Prayer of Presence would piece by piece reveal what happened at the moment of my "yes."The angel immediately handed the gift to Jesus and Mike. The gift floated in mid-air and unwrapped. A glowing globe of light shedding white and colored rays lit up the room. Then Mike, with Jesus superimposed within him, took the sparkling light and gently pushed it into my heart.

After Mike left for Phoenix, the following morning I rose early and tried this new kind of prayer. Before anyone woke, I took a shot of coffee and slipped into a faintly lit chapel. It was my first experiment with this "image-prayer-thing." I'd planned to merely test the waters with my big toe, but tripped and splashed head over heels into the pool.

Breaking from tradition, I sat there bookless, no prayer book, no meditation book. Heaven forbid! Praying without a prayerbook in hand! Just solitude and silence. A pulsating sanctuary flame danced on the walls. I settled into a comfortable chair and closed my eyes. The house was still asleep. Totally unexpected, a powerful image thrust itself into my mind. Its force and graphic details startled me.

I found myself standing on an elevated hill of great height. Ankle-high green grass swayed thick all around. My feet were firmly set upon a cobblestone road that stretched downward and straight ahead disappearing over the distant and vast horizon. A golden sunset lit up the whole valley before me, painting a thread of road with reflected light. A light breeze flowed over me. I stood there awestruck at the sheer beauty of the sprawling scene.

I had no idea where this image originated. I hadn't planned its creation, nor tried to construct it. It just appeared in my mind, or soul, entirely whole and intact. The more I searched its content with closed eyes, the more details I discovered.

While gazing ahead, thoroughly enjoying the panorama, I suddenly realized that Jesus stood next to me in the scene. He also enjoyed the beauty of the moment. While we gazed into the distance, he gently took my hand in his. His left hand; my right. My heart jumped, my heart not in the scene but in my real body. I was lost in the beauty of the scene and the presence of Jesus. My real body and emotions reacted. Then Jesus said something: "Here is the best part of your life, Andy."

It felt like those words came from behind my right shoulder and from the deepest, most mysterious place within me. He and his words were both outside and inside me. I sat there in the chapel and cried. I believed everything. I understood that I was about to walk that road and be transformed. The experience was overwhelming. So, this was prayer? I experienced the intimacy and comfort of a real relationship with Jesus. I experienced his touch and a genuine conversation, even if only a few words from his lips. My life would never be the same again.

By the time the community trickled in for formal morning prayers in Latin, I was hooked. The meditation had seized me. I felt instantly addicted. That first-time experience filled a vacuum of beauty and meaning deep inside me. By the time community prayers finished, I exited the chapel that morning with an unaccustomed feeling of hope. I bumped around that day with a vague disorientation and anticipation of good things to come.

14

INTIMATE FULLNESS

The "filling of the reservoir," the "up-grading of the heart" now took place. After two years and ten months, about a thousand prayer experiences later, I became an entirely different person. If the overflow be understood, you must first grasp the filling of the reservoir: the filling of my soul with Jesus.

Never missing a day, I woke faithfully to an early hour of hidden prayer. The best hour of the day! I learned the art of how to be still and receive like a coddled infant. Notice how the infant does hardly anything but passively surrender to another's love. Yes, I used to describe the Prayer of Presence as "Baby Meditation." And so it is, from the perspective of what you do. Pretty much nothing.

I stopped begging for help, reading, introspecting, trying to learn, and making resolutions to be a better person. I abandoned the indoctrination that love is only defined by outward action. The focus of prayer shifted from the duty or achievement of giving love, to simply surrendering to love received. Giving love begins with receiving love. I had to experience that phase in life before the maturity of giving would one day appear. I just pictured Jesus loving me and soaked in his face, his touch, his warm accepting companionship. His love rushed into me and changed everything. Prayer was no longer my work, but his.

I lived a day-by-day journey of love, absorbed in Jesus' long planned world of images in my heart. Each day birthed a fresh dimension of rescue and resurrection in my soul. Life was like hanging onto a speeding locomotive. Fifteen months later, I did reach that painful intensity of love that Mike described. Feeling like I was exploding with happiness on the inside, I could barely receive more love! It gushed into me like a torrent!

The filling of my soul was so comprehensive and profound I can barely scratch the surface what took hold of me. Each advancement was linked to a scene with Jesus that told its own story. Often, organically linked scenes and stories lasted for several days, until God completed an aspect of my rescue and development. He'd then move on to my next need, and his next step to transform me for purposes I couldn't image. I had no plan but to receive. After suffering for my entire adult life, I now knew how to pray!

During this receiving period Jesus' presence radically penetrated the foundational pillars of my life. I can only offer a glimpse of what he did. Otherwise, there's just way too much to cover. But I'll try to abridge the fruits of the gift of prayer that flourished within.

Hope was the first thing that happened. I had forgotten what that felt like. Such a wonderful feeling now! It held me, wrapped its arms around me, soothed me with abiding peace. Jesus' presence welcomed me each morning and I felt happy to wake up now. Amazing, because I woke each morning confined in the brutal environment of a cult. I lived in two different worlds: an ugly outer environment, and an inner beautiful paradise. And my "heart-world" became more real to me.

Gradually, the grip of vice lost its tenacious hold on my heart. My attractions to pornography, masturbation, and alcohol abuse weakened. The attracting power of sin eventually faded away. I'd found a better "coping pleasure" in life: the innermost enjoyment of a Divine Person who loved me. Moral sensitivity appeared. I used to judge morality primarily in mechanical terms of breaking laws or not. Now, my heart played an overriding role in my moral life. I judged the goodness of my acts according to how genuinely I loved Jesus and my neighbor. I shifted from check marking conformity to laws to loving others in the best way possible.

Gradually, Jesus took me to many traumatic scenes in my past. We watched them together. My soul vomited a lot of evil hauntings. I cried a lot. I got mad, I complained; I felt the despair and confusion of those terrible moments. Then I suddenly saw him there, working his love.

He was actually there in each instance. I saw his presence! I understood him allowing the evil for a wonderful suffering that would draw me to him. After multiple wild journeys into my past, Jesus healed me of every traumatic memory. All the trauma in my life was well worth the love I now enjoy.

Gradually, the continuous receiving of Jesus' love made me grow up emotionally. The speed and power of this change made me feel my inner emotions; love and joy filled me. Mask wearing, fear, timidity, dread, frustration, despondency, and stagnation all steadily faded away. I had once referred to the Prayer of Presence as "therapeutic prayer." Yes of course, this kind of prayer makes you grow up and heals your soul.

I finally felt what it was like to have a real friend. I discovered how to bare my soul, speak with raw sincerity, and feel the security of a friend's hand. Oh, how I had longed for a genuine friend in life! Heartfelt emotional strength resulted from the experience of Jesus' personal love for me.

My lightning-speed emotional development reached a wonderful human peak. I experienced the "psychic birth" I had missed in life. Emotional growth finally led me to discover my own intrinsic value and worth. I did not need others to confirm this value, nor did I need to convince myself of my worth, nor did I need to desperately work to be accepted. I knew my own independent goodness. I was loved and lovable regardless of others' confirmation. I knew and felt my inherent goodness by Jesus' unconditional acceptance and love for me. My intellect and emotions agreed that I was worthy of God's love.

Jesus' love and truth are inseparable. He is Love. He is Truth. Accordingly, as Jesus' love filled me so did his truth. He had healed my memories, developed healthy emotions, and matured my morals and self-perception. Next, he moved on to the renewal of my mind. I had discovered what is good or harmful for my soul. Now I began to judge my environment through God's eyes.

Friendship with Jesus taught me that I lived in a harmful environment. It deprived me from true prayer and therefore from an intimate relationship with Jesus. It conditioned me to live in fear. It indoctrinated me to deny my own goodness and specialness in Jesus' eyes. It perverted my perception about what was good or harmful to me. My new way of praying gradually led me to discard a toxic environment and embrace an entirely new paradigm of life.

Jesus didn't stop there. Once my emotions strengthened and my good judgment prevailed, the intimacy of prayer brought on courage and power to break free from captivity. Now I had a healthy self-love and stood firm. I didn't care what others thought about the path I assumed to free myself. Jesus told me in my prayer what to do. Just as much, he bestowed courage upon me. Love blossomed into conviction and power. Yes, profound love can be a threat to others because it clothes with bold power to confront evil and pursue good.

I remember the scariest moment of my life. I had locked myself in a basement bathroom, crying because of the harsh environment that sometimes got to me. As my head rested on the floor, I felt Jesus' hand on my back. He bent down and whispered in my ear, "Andy, go to the Vatican and report everything that is happening here." That scared me because of my house confinement. It meant that I had to secretly escape from the house.

I was certain Jesus asked me to do this. Yet I hesitated, saying, "But what would it do? I don't know anybody there." He answered, "I will reveal my friends there." I found the courage in him to venture forth that very morning. I ended up submitting 89 pages of sworn testimony to the Vatican regarding my entrapment in the cult. Only growth in genuine prayer gave me the truth and power to do the right thing. I'm sitting here today writing to you because of this.

My love story with Jesus continues. The Prayer of Presence kept filling me with intimacy and leading me through unexpected frontiers, both interior and exterior. Prayer led me to leave the cult, the country, the Catholic priesthood, and embrace marriage, fatherhood, and a salaried job. Everything was new to me. I hope this summary adequately describes the filling of my soul.

15

SOME FRUITS OF THE PRAYER OF PRESENCE

1. The ending of serious sins, even addictions

2. A profound self-understanding and knowledge of the lies believed about oneself

3. An overwhelming sense of peace and intimacy

4. The healing of traumatic memories

5. Profound emotional and psychological development

6. A gradual curing of anxieties, guilt, and fears

7. The emergence of hope and a healthy self-love and self-identity

8. A revelation of the good and bad elements in one's personal environment

9. Abiding friendship with Jesus

10. The capacity to forgive others

11. Great power and courage to confront evil

12. A new identity and purpose: beginning to know and live one's ultimate purpose in life

13. True holiness

14. The unexpected grace of prophetic gifts for the good of others

16

GIFT OVERFLOW

A quick review: We likened a person's special gift to a reservoir. God imparts the gift to enrich the person with goodness and then to overflow. I told you about my natural disposition of a good heart and the upgrading of it with the Prayer of Presence. We defined this special gift, described it, and briefly clarified how to practice it. Lastly, I revealed how I had received it through brokenness and how this gift enriched me. Now we're ready to talk about overflow.

Once the reservoir is filled to the brim it starts to overflow for the benefit of multitudes downstream. I had asked Jesus how to explain this organic development of the Prayer of Presence. He answered by sending me to the moment I'd first received the gift. He said, "Everything you need to say is there." So, after exploring the moment of rescue from the perspective of receiving and subsequent filling, we now consider that same moment from the perspective of Mike's overflow.

The moment I said "yes" to the Prayer of Presence an unseen world happened! Symbols are tricky things. They can be held flatly in a superficial manner. Or their meaning can be penetrated with a bit of reflection and a spark of God's grace. For instance, a child may see the flag as an arrangement of colors, but a veteran may see beyond the stars and stripes and feel the rush of liberty. The human spirit symbolizes, as the Divine Spirit does masterfully. The stillness of prayer unveils everything. It allows God to whisper.

Receiving the gift of prayer hinged upon my "yes." At the instant my soul surrendered, an angel handed Mike the gift. Ministerial angels offer assistance when the balance of eternal destiny shifts. There are few gifts greater than a commitment to genuine prayer. An angel then participated in the holy work of affecting an intimate friendship with Jesus. Angelic activity encouraged the giving of heaven's prayer-gift.

I saw the gift as a beautifully wrapped present. The gift symbolizes the capacity, knowledge, and inclination to true prayer. It floats in the air and unwraps in a hands-off fashion to unveil that it's not the product of my own efforts, but God's work. It's a gift, meaning that it's freely bestowed by God. It's a surprise neither expected nor deserved, nor the result of something due by labor. Its beautiful wrapping means that this heavenly grace now appears attractive, enticing, and welcoming.

As the wrapping falls away, a powerful sparking ball of light suspends in the air. Its rays of light shine everywhere and brighten the entire room. This is the light who is God, about to enter my life. Colored, moving flashes symbolize the dynamism and vibrancy of new life just before me.

Yet, the most astounding image is the placing of the gift. Mike holds the mini-sunshine, but Jesus is superimposed in Mike. When Mike moves, Jesus moves. When Jesus moves, Mike moves. So, it's a mutual act as the gift is pushed gently into my heart. This explains the wild, unmanageable overflow of the gift of the Prayer of Presence in Mike's own heart. He couldn't contain the gift. It had to be given. Overwhelming love enters new hearts as it expands. Jesus and Mike together placed the gift.

I say they acted together in a very specific way. Jesus himself was the primary cause, whereas Mike was the instrumental cause of placing the prayer gift. For instance, when a baseball slugger slams a homerun, it's the ballplayer who primarily causes the home run, not the bat. The bat is the instrumental cause. Similarly, Jesus himself places the gift of prayer in my heart, but through the use of Mike as a cooperating human instrument doing God's work. In this specific way, they worked together.

Although this clarifies who did what when placing the gift, overflow is truly about holiness more than anything else. Holiness is about God grabbing hold of a person and making that person his own in an intimate way. Through prayer this had taken place in Mike's soul and it reflected in his face.

It was not so much Mike's "doing" but his "being" that resulted in my receiving. At its deepest level, overflow is mostly about radiating friendship with Jesus. Holiness itself pulsates a spiritual-magnetic pull without the human instrument working much at all. Holiness draws and warms like a fire. People feel when another person is close to God, and somehow intimacy invites to intimacy. This mysterious reality certainly played a role in my receiving of the gift of prayer. Overflow then is God at work drawing souls to himself, but through the instrumentality of a close friend.

Mike's happy and compassionate face and new boldness said everything I needed to hear. He was once broken but now whole. The love of God did this, and it drew me to desire the same. Hardly anything speaks with more clarity and strength than the witness of a transformed life. Like a perfectly fitting glove, the Prayer of Presence then seems best fit for broken souls, passed on by a once broken soul. At least, that's how it played out for me.

Notwithstanding the many ways God intervenes in the lives and events of this world, the irresistible word of a holy man spoken into the ear of God is one of them. As such, the power of prayer is the power of friendship. Jesus listens to his friends. Mike's overflow began long before that Chicago meeting. Thousands of miles away, many months past, Mike had often prayed for me. Jesus responded with an unlikely day, place, and time to rescue me. Accordingly, overflow starts with praying for another person. God and his angels finish the job when the appointed moment comes.

17

DAILY PRAYER

Although an initial "yes" to the Prayer of Presence is critical, the habit of prayer must follow. A mere "yes" is not enough for the transformative process of prayer to sink roots in the soul. The "purchase" of a home often compels monthly payments to a mortgage company. Wedding vows demand an adjusted daily routine freshly mindful of another person. The prayer life is similar. The commitment to prayer implies an "investment" in a new daily habit. Once that good habit takes hold, long-lasting benefits flourish.

The pursuit of any worthwhile dream requires consistent effort. While the "yes" is essential, it's only the beginning. A nurse must first study every day to receive her license to practice. A professional violinist must practice every day if he's to get anywhere in the world of music. The gift of prayer is something supernatural, but its headway does hinge upon a daily human habit. Practice makes perfect. Of course, God can impart a habit instantly, but he cherishes the faith-filled path of personal determination.

I must soberly weigh my values, then. What's most important to me? What should I keep? What should I either eliminate or shelve to schedule prayer time? Where can I give up something to make room for an hour of daily prayer? This will take soul searching. I'll need to swap something I like for something better. And then it takes courage to step forward with a serious commitment.

So, I don't have time? Time is relative. If a doctor says I have six months to live, suddenly I have time. Consider when a person finds the love of his life. Wouldn't that man cut every corner to find the time to be with the other? Such a radical value shift is needed. A meaningful relationship takes time. If I want a future with someone, I must spend time with that person. It's the same with Jesus. I must sit with him, walk, share dreams and feelings, hold hands, and listen, if a real friendship is to have a chance.

Commitment can be a scary word. But there's no way around it. Building a relationship with God takes a time investment. Upon your knees, your commitment needs to be thought through, deliberate, and expressed out loud to Jesus. Promise your time. You know that time investment is necessary to human achievements. Just apply it to prayer. There's no messing around here. No commitment, no progress.

I'd committed myself twice in life to a daily hour of the Prayer of Presence. The first time I said "yes" was when I sat before Father Mike in Chicago in October 2005. I knew I had to commit myself right then and there. No consideration or measurement was made to figure out how. Desperation would somehow find a way to make it work.

A couple of days later I experienced my first Prayer of Presence meditation. Perhaps that first time might be described as an activation of the gift. Distinguish here between receiving a gift and using it. For instance, knowing about someone is vastly different from actually living with that person. The gift is knowing how to pray and feeling drawn to it but praying is the use of the gift. I can be gifted with a fishing pole and a booklet on how to fish, but fishing is a dramatic splash from theory to practice.

After about a thousand life-changing meditations, the regularity and intensity of my prayer life faded. I gradually, unfortunately allowed the interests and concerns of human life to overshadow the time I spent with Jesus. The Prayer of Presence was reduced to in-between moments here and there, still occasionally beneficial but diminished in scope and power.

The liberty and details of human life just happened. Somehow, life inadvertently translated into less time for prayer. I'm sure everybody understands this. I had escaped from a cult, penned 89 pages of sworn statements for the Vatican, fled to multiple countries, obtained a laicization from the Catholic priesthood, got married, had kids, authored a memoir, settled into a full-time job, and bought a house. Twelve busy years slipped by, and I'd foolishly buried the treasure of my prayer life.

God wisely allows suffering to nudge the soul to pray. So wise! Sadly, when we're content in life the need and hunger for God diminishes. I'd grown up, broke free from tyranny, escaped Rome, and settled into married life. Generally happy and preoccupied, I prayed less.

In March 2020, I committed myself to a daily hour of prayer again. Two weeks in a hospital brought me to my knees again. I'll share that story later. It's enough to say here that this second time I committed myself to a daily hour or prayer was more difficult than the first. I was considerably more involved and distracted with the minutiae of human life.

I lived a jam-packed life: full-time work, a wife and family, property and car, bills to pay, endless errands, continuous attempts to secure more income. But I felt Jesus calling me back to an hour of daily prayer. I knew I had to do it. So, I scrutinized my daily schedule and decided to sacrifice something I loved.

I love writing. It's my passion. I believed I had to have it. It fulfilled a deep need within me for processing and meaningful creativity. It seemed so essential. Without it I tended to be frustrated and grumpy. Writing satisfied an emotional need to discover, understand and share. It even compensated for a general state of sexual frustration in my life. Writing was an indispensable pleasure for me.

An early bird, I'd rise early to write, then wake the family and tackle the workday. I knew what I had to do. I committed myself to get up around three or four in the morning and devote myself to prayer. I replaced writing with prayer. Jesus expressed his pleasure of my determined choice and assured me that the time would come when I'd write again, when he urges. That's why I write now, but not at the expense of lost prayer. I'm now about 500 meditations into my second Prayer of Presence venture.

18

TRAGEDY & DESTINY

After a third futile visit to the urgent care clinic, Olha, the kids and I reluctantly arrived at the emergency entrance of a hospital in Phoenix, Arizona. During the past month, three antibiotic treatments had utterly failed. A painful and creeping wound seized my right foot, and I could barely walk now. We tried to pinch pennies, but finally confronted the ugly reality: either keep attempting to save money and lose my foot or save the foot and worry about expenses later.

A kindhearted nurse introduced me to a wheelchair. I didn't like the feeling of losing my mobility and independence at all! My blood sugar blinked at 450. Surprise: I had an acute diabetic foot ulcer requiring urgent surgery. It was the evening of December 30, 2019. I wouldn't be wheeled out of the hospital until two weeks later, $240,000 in debt, but with my foot intact. Two surgeries amputated the small toe and a side portion of my right foot. A rude awakening to 2020, the best year of my life.

At 58 years old, life was reasonably comfortable and fulfilling. I enjoyed a wonderful wife and two amazing young boys. A decent and meaningful job greeted me every morning. Our family even relished living in our own home, albeit mostly owned by the mortgage bank, but it did feel like ours anyway. Though my spiritual life no longer thrived, I persevered with a less intense relationship with God.

Honestly, I was more scared of the anesthesia than losing a chunk of my foot. Familiar with possible surgical tragedies, I prepared to die before each operation. I repented, begged for eternal salvation, and asked Jesus if I could keep living with at least three toes. With a hug and a kiss, I shared the confident state of my soul with Olha, just in case I'd die. In a worst-case scenario, I didn't want my wife guessing about my eternal salvation for the rest of her life. I hugged each of my boys, 10 and 8 years, and told them I loved them from the bottom of my heart.

After the hospital ordeal, I spent a couple of months in bed, often lulled to sleep by the hum of a wound-vac machine. With plenty of time to reflect, my mortality hit me deeply. I could have died! I became alarmed. What was I doing with my life? I was a decent, kind fellow, but living far short of God's intentions for me in this world.

I'd imagine myself in heaven a billion years into the future. A persistent question kept pressing upon my soul. "In God's eternal eyes, did I fulfill the ultimate purpose why he created me and placed me upon the earth?" The same answer kept emerging from the gut of my spirit: "No! Not yet! Now is the moment then to finally do what I was created to do."

I knew what I had to do. Jesus granted me the clarity and courage to again commitment myself to an hour of prayer every morning, like old times. Washed with tears, I repented of not taking my prayer seriously. Naked, just as I was born into this world, seeing Jesus in my mind as my head touched the floor, I made a solemn vow to resume my prayer walk.

I've committed many long lasting and damaging sins in life. I had indulged for years in pornography and masturbation, given up on life, despaired and rejected God, slept with another man's wife, lost my trust and hope in God, lived absorbed in mere material horizons. A profuse and bitter eruption of tears streamed down my face when I grasped the worst sin of my life. It was none of these things. Jesus had given me the gift of prayer and I had abandoned it. I had received the treasure of my life and for twelve years stuck it on a shelf to collect dust. That realization hurt me to the core. Truly, what a sin! The sin of doing nothing with such a special gift!

I ventured earnestly again on the path of prayer. Like riding a bike, you never forget how to pray. A deluge of spiritual riches washed into every part of my soul. The grace was so immediate and plentiful it felt like I'd never missed a beat. Jesus gave no corrections or stern warnings. He simply hugged me and smiled, saying, "Andy, where have you been? I missed you." He is pure love!

This second time around, my prayer was both the same and very different. It was the same in nurturing friendship and intimacy, but different in God's intentions and direction in my life. Simply put, my previous experience of prayer was mostly about receiving love and growing up. Presuming emotional and spiritual development, everything now shifted to giving. The overflow of love took over. So different than before! I lived an explosion of love inside!

My heart always burns to love people and teach them how to pray. I'm very determined about my destiny to save millions of people. Finally, I'm living the life I was created for. By Jesus' urging, I fasted on water for 40 days begging for the grace to powerfully impart love and prayer into countless souls. I believe I'm now living his answer. He knows I'm serious. He's making me his prayer warrior!

Don't fear or run away from suffering; it has its place to transform you. First it will make you compassionate and grant meaning in your life. Tragedy can push you to your destiny to truly love with great power. Personal prayer can teach you more about God, the world, and yourself than any book, even this one.

19

SOME PRAYER OF PRESENCE BIBLE INFERENCES

1. "But when you pray, go into your room and shut the door and pray to your father who is in secret; and your Father who sees in secret will reward you." Matthew 6:6

2. "...your Father knows what you need before you ask him." Matthew 6:8

3. "Come to me, all who labor and are heavy laden, and I will give you rest." Matthew 11:28

4. "...a great while before day, he rose and went out to a lonely place, and there he prayed." Mark 1:35

5. "In this is love, not that we loved God but that he loved us..." I John 4:10

6. "We love, because he first loved us." I John 4:19

7. "...love the Lord your God with all your heart, and with all your soul, and with all your mind." Matt. 22:37

8. "This people honors me with their lips, but their heart is far from me." Matthew 15:8

9. "If any one thirst, let him come to me and drink. He who believes in me, as the scripture has said, 'out of his heart shall flow rivers of living water.'" John 7:37-39

10. "Whoever drinks of the water that I shall give him will become in him a spring of water welling up to eternal life." John 4:14

11. "That the God of our Lord Jesus Christ, the Father of glory, may give you a spirit of wisdom and of revelation in the knowledge of him, having the eyes of your hearts enlightened..." Ephesians 1:17-18

12. "I thank you Father, Lord of heaven and earth, that you have hidden these things from the wise and understanding and revealed them to infants." Matthew 11:25

13. "Truly, I say to you, whoever does not receive the kingdom of God like a child shall not enter it." Luke 18:17

14. "Blessed are those who have not seen and yet believe." John 20:29

15. God's presence was neither in the strong wind, earthquake, nor fire, but in "a still whisper." 1 Kings 19:12

20

SPIRITUAL AUTHORITY

I could share hundreds of marvelous prayer experiences but hesitate. I've had my share. They would stir up some good feelings, but I believe they'd hold you back. You'd feel that such prayer is beyond you, or you would try to imitate my path. No, you must discover your own way. Jesus has personal revelations and a unique gift reserved just for you. You be the one to surprise me in heaven!

There's one thing left that you should know in advance about your future. Be faithful in prayer and Jesus will enter you, fill you, and make you an instrument in his hands to save countless souls. You may feel weak now, but on an unexpected day in the future the power of God's love will lead you like a general into battle. In him, you will come to know exactly who you are. And you'll be able to do what is impossible now. Little by little, I'm getting there. I'll share only one prayer experience that explains this.

I was in my prayer-gift room in heaven. As I stood there amidst the angels at the wrapping table, I skimmed the names on the opened page of the massive book. Temporarily, Jesus seemed to leave me alone to learn things from my assigned angels. I'd learned how to send angels in prayer, how to use the sword of the spirit, how to impart prayer-gifts in hearts, and a lot more.

I started to thumb through the book and asked about a certain person. Let's call him John. I urgently desired for John to receive his prayer-gift soon. He needed it so badly! So, I asked where John was listed. An angel then showed me the name deep in the book, meaning that the gift would not be received for a very long time. Seeing the name so distant in time upset me: "No, this is not acceptable! This person needs to learn how to pray right now!" The angels stared silently, as if they couldn't do anything about it.

I opened to that future page and somehow slipped my hand in between the name and the paper, pealing "John" off into my hand. That surprised me. Then I flipped a thick volume of pages and pressed his name within the margin of the front page. The name actually stuck. Cool, I thought. The delivery and reception of the prayer-gift was now advanced considerably. I felt good about that. The angels didn't say anything.

Suddenly, Jesus stood behind me to my right. He saw what I did. Busted! I thought I'd get in trouble. I turned to him, and he said, "You can't do that." I don't know from where it came from inside of me, but I answered, "Yes, I can." We stared into each other's eyes. That moment of silence seemed like an eternity. Everything froze. Then, Jesus gently placed his hand upon my shoulder and smiled ever so slightly. He did not break his gaze into my eyes. He softly said, "Andy, you are learning." Wow, did that feel good! Something profoundly changed in me.

The instant he spoke, a torrent of understanding filled my mind. It was like a compact and instantaneous download. Jesus made me understand that my prayer-gift room is like a family business. He's ultimately in charge. But when he's out, I'm in charge. By his authority I make decisions, transact business, and speak on his behalf. He assumes I have his delegated authority to act in his name. He wants me to act on that authority. He desires to advance anyone to receive the gift of prayer and certainly approves my actions to do the same. He expects me to take charge of my room and lead my angels in his work of saving souls. He's training and teaching me. I grasped all of these details in a flash of awareness. It was an incredible teaching moment for me.

Spiritual authority grows from intimate prayer. For clarity's sake, it's not the same as church authority. It's not the exercise of authority by an appointed church official. Rather, spiritual authority is confidently acting in unison with Jesus' own authority. He acts and you act together dispelling evil and calling forth something beneficial for souls. Healing and revealing hidden truths are connected to the use of this authority. As my prayer advances, this seems to be the next area of development Jesus has in mind. Good prayer always pushes us to new frontiers for the salvation of souls.

CONCLUSION

For the last few mornings, Jesus has urged me to conclude. After writing now for a few months, a deluge of ideas percolate. They're swirling around in my soul searching for a way to burst out. There's a lot more to say. I'm exploding with the desire to explain more, to reveal more, to explain the treasure of my prayer life. I've only scratched the surface. No doubt I could write a thousand pages more of the love poured into me and the mysteries revealed.

I feel and know, and even hear the desire and instructions of Jesus: "Andy, it's enough. We're finished." I sense an urgency about his words, repeated for a few mornings now. He stands next to me as I type. I say to him: "Please conclude for me. How would you like to end things?" He moves beside me and then within me and I hear him say:

"People may admire whatever more you could say, but that will never be enough. You've obeyed and said what was necessary. Every soul is unique and special to me. Our purpose is just to open a door and invite. I infinitely love each reader and hold out my hand. My dear reader, it's now your turn to step through the doorway and live your own miracles with me."

Amen

Morning Prayer

Come, oh Holy Trinity. Here I am before your infinity. Immersed in your timeless eternity, limitless knowledge, boundless presence before all creation, in awe I humbly bow down and worship you. Who am I so small to be bathed in the sparkling rays of your immensity?

You're the blinding brightness of truth, infinite power of love gushing like a raging river. In your immutable mind, you're beginningless and endless knowing, willing, creating, loving. I'm so unworthy to be in your presence; yet here you are! I worship you.

Father, Son, and Holy Spirit you surround me and dwell pleasurably within me. I can hardly grasp this beautiful reality! How I worship and love you! May the power of your truth and healing radiate from my heart and illuminate the multitudes you bring to yourself --in my hidden soul.

Oh, my breathtaking friend Jesus, here's my hand. Walk me into the overwhelming mystery of your uncreated, all-powerful family. Lead me to broken souls, bring them to me today. Let them see and feel you inside me. Let their hearts surrender to your family's personal presence attracting them, appealing to them through my body and soul.

Jesus, I ask you to grant each soul understanding, healing, and the sweet gift of your intimate friendship in our wonderous world of prayer. Let your lost sheep see your face in mine.

Amen

AUTHOR'S NOTE

Flashy books need prestigious publishing houses, clever marketing platforms, and targeted celebrity endorsements to dominate a best seller list. Jesus needs none of this. He loves to fly beneath the radar, invisibly at work in marginalized souls. Let prayer fill you with love. Then let your love overflow.

Todd Scott received the gift of the Prayer of Presence about 20 years ago. Ever since, with wonderful spiritual fruits, he masterfully teaches how to practice it. He once taught Fr. Michael Dietrich. (Another amazing story.) Mike then introduced me to the Prayer of Presence. Todd and I have been friends for 34 years.

I refuse income from this book. Profit is not the point. I wrote only because Jesus told me to write. No doubt, he wants you to discover the depths of prayer. You hold the secret of powerful prayer in your hands. Read it. Learn it. Pray! Let your prayer life transform you. Then let love take over. Spread the gift.

You have my permission to copy, publish, and post this book as you wish. Photocopy a few for family members. Read to the sick. Give to the broken-hearted. Share a photocopy with your prayer group, minister, co-worker, or best friend. You've received freely; freely give.

Some may feel the invitation of Jesus to do more. I encourage you to publish as you desire and spread this book through blogs, emails, websites, and social media platforms. I'll gladly provide the files you may need, for free.

Just ask:

West Valley
Andrew Lee Sullivan
P. O. Box 43012
Phoenix, Arizona 85080
howtopray.andy@gmail.com

East Valley
Todd Scott
howtopray.todd@gmail.com

If you or your friends need personal instructions on how to pray as proposed in this book, reach out to Todd or me. We'll do whatever we can to help. Perhaps Jesus may urge you to gather a group to learn how to practice the Prayer of Presence.

Todd Scott is the author of *Quenching the Soul's Thirst*: a practical step by step guide to the practice of the Prayer of Presence. His book may be purchased through www.bbgnes.com/qst. I'm the author of *Vatican Intervention*: my personal testimony of how Jesus Christ rescued me through the Prayer of Presence. My book may be purchased through Amazon.com.

If you believe this booklet would help many people, please send a donation to the above P.O. Box, with an enclosed check made out to Andrew Lee Sullivan, or send your help through PayPal to howtopray.andy@gmail.com. Without personal profit, donations will be used to print and distribute this booklet far and wide.

Love and prayers,
Andrew Lee Sullivan
Phoenix, Arizona
January 12, 2022w